The Other White House

Ceneca VanTassell – Luto
Illustrated by E. Jackie Brown

AuthorHouse™
1663 Liberty Drive
Bloomington, IN 47403
www.authorhouse.com
Phone: 1-800-839-8640

First published by AuthorHouse   3/11/2011

ISBN: 978-1-4567-4052-8 (sc)

Library of Congress Control Number: 2011906239

Printed in the United States of America

Certain stock imagery © Thinkstock.

This book is printed on acid-free paper.

authorHOUSE®

8-26-11
To All the Grandchildren who Grew Up in a Different White House, I hope you enjoy reading about my special white house. ☺

Cindy

Dedication

I am very lucky to have had such wonderful grandparents. They were special, yet humble, people and I couldn't have had the life I've had if it wasn't for Grandpa and Grandma Millis.

I cherish the memories of my grandparents' white farmhouse. I hope you have a special place to cherish also.

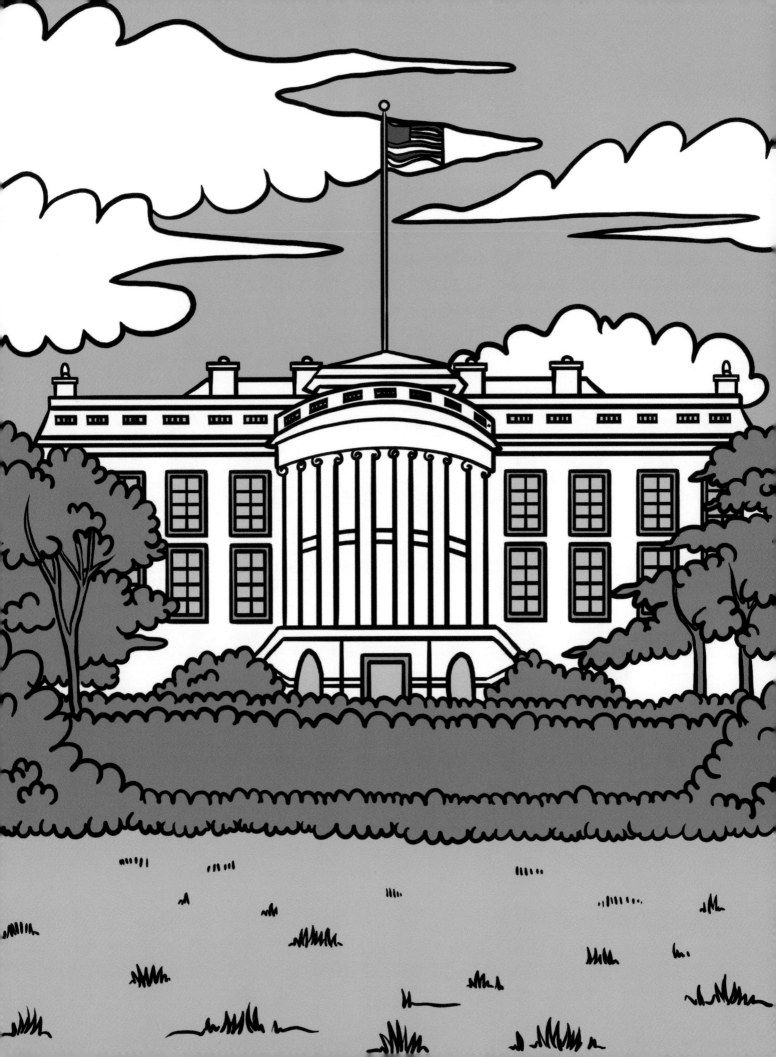

We all know the White House at 1600 Pennsylvania Avenue. It's home to the President and his family.

The White House was built in 1792. All of the presidents, except George Washington, have enjoyed living in this house of few.

The White House is many a stately places. The big White House entertains from all races.

I have been to the White House. It sits so majestic for all to see. There is, though, another white house that sits as majestic as can be. You ask, "What house would that be?"

This white house is special to me. It was built in 1863. No presidents have stayed here. No famous people have slept here, just my family and me.

My grandparents bought this white house in 1933. There are no fancy pictures on the walls, just pictures of my family and me.

The Presidential White House has 132 rooms to see. My special white house has only 10 rooms, which is enough for me. There's one special room in this white house that's important to me. My mother was born in that room you see.

A grand staircase at the White House was built for all to view. The banister of wrought iron and wood with carpet a reddish hue. Many important people walk the staircase through.

The grand staircase, at the other white house, is a wooden humble one, but oh, what fun! My sister, cousins, and I slide down and down and go round and round.

The big White House has a Rose Garden and many different flowers. My grandparents' white house has a vegetable garden where they spend many hours.

The big White House sits on 18 acres of land. The city of Washington D.C. surrounds the house as planned. 1600 Pennsylvania Avenue is a busy place. The presidents refer to it as home base.

The other white house sits so proud on 50 acres of soil. The crops each year surround the house so loyal.

Traditionally, the White House has a pedigree pet. The other white house has a dog, no papers or pedigree, but the best dog you ever met. Max is always by my Grandpa's side befriending him with such pride.

At the Presidential White House, important people are invited to many a fancy dinner. The table is long and beautifully set. The kitchen is a buzz with many helping hands. The elegant dinner is served. It is the best yet.

The other white house has a kitchen so small. There's only 1 cook, that's all. My Grandma fixes dinners like no other, except for maybe my mother. The table is set with Grandma's dishes, the ones from her wedding wishes.

While visiting my grandparents' house each time, I would find life in the country so sublime.

Tourists flock by the thousands to tour the big White House. They stand behind ropes with many things to view.

The other white house was open for family and friends too. The view at the other white house is certain to behold. My grandparent's things are wonderfully old.

Tourists will remember their visit to the Presidential White House come what may. But in my mind, I visit my grandparents' white house everyday!

Author's page

The Other White House is Ceneca Luto's first published book. The author is a 4th grade teacher and has shared many stories of her grandparent's farm with her students over 29 years in the classroom.

Ceneca Luto is a National Board Certified teacher in Crystal Lake, Illinois. She lives there with her husband, son and daughter. Ceneca enjoys writing, traveling and spending time with her family and friends.

CPSIA information can be obtained
at www.ICGtesting.com

230530LV00002BC